Guided Meditation for Anxiety and Kundalini Awakening

(2 in 1)

Align Your Chakras, Awaken Your Third Eye, Reduce Stress and Anxiety, Find Inner Peace, and Heal Your Soul

PUBLISHED BY: Kaizen Mindfulness Meditations

© Copyright 2019 - All rights reserved.

The content contained within this book may not be reproduced, duplicated or transmitted without direct written permission from the author or the publisher.

Under no circumstances will any blame or legal responsibility be held against the publisher, or author, for any damages, reparation, or monetary loss due to the information contained within this book. Either directly or indirectly.

Legal Notice:

This book is copyright protected. This book is only for personal use. You cannot amend, distribute, sell, use, quote or paraphrase any part, or the content within this book, without the consent of the author or publisher.

Disclaimer Notice:

Please note the information contained within this document is for educational and entertainment purposes only. All effort has been executed to present accurate, up to date, and reliable, complete information. No warranties of any kind are declared or implied. Readers acknowledge that the author is not engaging in the rendering of legal, financial, medical or professional advice. The content within this book has been derived from various sources. Please consult a licensed professional before attempting any techniques outlined in this book.

By reading this document, the reader agrees that under no circumstances is the author responsible for any losses, direct or indirect, which are incurred as a result of the use of information contained within this document, including, but not limited to, — errors, omissions, or inaccuracies

Table of Contents

Book #1: Meditation for Anxiety 4

I: Starting Off 5
II: Connect to the Pace of the Earth 9
III: Calm the Chaos 14
IV: Realize Your Path 18
V: Make Space for Health 22

Book #2: Meditation for Kundalini Awakening 26

I: Gather Your Energy 27
II: On the Kundalini 31
III: Your Inner Truth 35
IV: Visualizing & Making Space for Awakening 39
V: What's to Come 43

Thank you 47

Guided Meditation for Anxiety and Kundalini Awakening

Meditation for Anxiety

Self-Hypnosis and Guided Imagery for Stress Relief, Boost Confidence and Inner Peace and Reduce Depression with Mindfulness and Positive Affirmations

I: Starting Off

As you take hold of this moment and begin your journey into meditation, you should feel proud and grateful for you've decided to take your health into your own hands. Congratulations on doing so. By coming to this meditation, in particular, you've decided to work against the intense force of anxiety in your life and you've decided to invite your personal potential to grow, to change for the better. To make the most of this experience, you must start off by calming yourself and collecting your energy. The first step in completing this important task involves assuming the correct position.

If you're able to, come to a comfortable seated position. If you don't have time to sit, first of all, don't worry – this won't take long. In fact, this exercise should feel relaxing and self-assuring rather than contributive to your overall anxiety and it won't take more than 10 minutes away from your focus on other things. If you don't have time to sit, simply stand and feel as relaxed as you can be. Release the weight of your shoulders, let go of any tension in your face, your arms, or your legs, and just allow yourself to feel loose. Allow yourself to feel open and ready to grow and get ready to fully begin.

Close your eyes if you can and if you're completing this exercise on the move, try to look at just one thing in particular as we proceed. In fact, as you can, look out *past* that thing you've chosen to focus on and then let what you're seeing fade from focus completely. You're trying to minimize the distractions around you so you can begin this meditation practice in earnest. Now, turn your attention to your breath, whether you're seated or standing, with eyes closed or open. Turn your attention to your breathing.

How is your respiration flowing now? As you begin to notice it more and more fully, can you tell? Is your breathing even? Is it steady and consistent? Is it deep and fulfilling? Or is it faltering and labored? Do you find yourself breathing without issue or do you accidentally hold your breath a lot? Notice the pace and quality of your breathing and then attempt to make it more consistent.

Consciously, follow each inhalation and exhalation. Imagine that you can see in your mind's eye the air that flows into your body through your nose and mouth, filling your lungs and belly, before exiting out through your mouth or nose once more. "Watch" as this respiration process happens and through the power of your focus, make each inhalation last three seconds and each exhalation last four. Breathe with the aid of this pattern and timing for at least 10 repetitions. If you can sustain this pattern, do so, but you can also simply shift away from that pattern to allow your breathing to assume a pace that's entirely natural to you – as long as it's even and deep and steady.

Once you've increased this conscious and healthy breathing, you'll be faced with the task of centering yourself. As soon as you've established this conscious, fulfilling breath pattern, you'll find it's much easier to determine your more profound and hidden opinions, hopes, thoughts, and feelings, but sometimes these things can distract us from the core of who we really are – the energy that centers us in this lifetime.

Pay attention now to those thoughts and feelings. You've linked with your breath and that breathing focus can always be used to regain traction when your thoughts and feelings become too much, but for now, do try to look directly at the action going on in your mind. What's going on emotionally? Are you feeling relatively neutral or is an emotion taking clear precedence for you? Are you overwhelmed right now or do things feel okay? As someone who suffers through anxiety on a daily basis, you might be coming to this meditation because you just need to prepare yourself for the day. However, you also might be coming to this meditation because you require immediate relief.

For now, just look at what's going on within you. If you're feeling overwhelmed or extremely emotional, breathe deeply for a few inhalations and exhalations. Breathe deeply and let yourself feel calm, confident, and securely safe in this meditative moment. Remind yourself that you really are safe and that the next few moments will help you feel sane, too. Remind yourself that you're working on healing *right now*. As your emotions zip around or stay still and linger around, let their intensity fade. Try to let your deep breathing dissolve any emotional intensities or triggers that may be holding you back from your highest potential. Try to breathe through and *past* these feelings.

Look too at the state of your thoughts. What's on your mind? With the emotion that's most clear to you, what thoughts surround that feeling? What circumstances do you think caused the feeling and thought-pool in the first place? As you can, examine and analyze your thoughts and see what's going on within you. Are your thoughts multiple and constant or are they slow and singular? Is there something particular holding your attention or is there no extra special one thing? As you note what's going on within, gather your knowledge then let it start to fade from attention once more.

In the space behind your conscious thoughts, your goals, and your fears – in the space behind your emotions and behind your eyes where imagination takes place – you find your true center. In this empty, neutral, still, and calm space, you can do and be anything you want to be. Call this your safe space, your happy place, the seat of your soul, or the source of your imagination – this space is where you can take note and begin healing yourself. Through careful attention on the breath and through the silencing of distracting thoughts and feelings, you connect with your center and are left with the singular opportunity of growth, expansion, and transformation.

II: Connect to the Pace of the Earth

With your breathing now constant and steady, with your mind now stilled and at peace, you are ready to connect to the pace of the earth. As someone with high anxiety or troubles interacting earnestly because of incessant concerns, worries, or panic attacks, you likely fight the pace of the earth despite how it constantly makes itself clear around you. Before you can fully heal yourself and fight back against those anxious tendencies, you'll have to reconnect with the pace of the natural and check yourself on what you've been fighting.

Anxious people have the tendency to desire, need, and/or demand control of their lives which causes strife because control is so hard to fully achieve. Anxious people will tend to force themselves to do certain things to decrease worry. They'll establish systems that need to be completed, rules that need to be met, and standards that need to be confirmed before they feel safe to expand or proceed. At the worst of times, anxious people will be *unable* to proceed unless their hopes of control are satisfied. In these ways, anxious people force themselves to work against the pace of the earth, in hopes of saving themselves.

Interestingly, the efforts of anxious people who get to this point go so fiercely against the forces and flows of nature that these individuals lose touch with the most basic principle of healing — the only way *out* is *through*. Anxious people will do well to remember that taking strife out of one's life completely rejects the natural flows of time and space. In fact, these people will come to make great leaps in healing only when they realize that "going with the flow" is about more than just letting things happen. The phrase is more so (and this is especially the case for highly anxious people) about getting in touch with natural patterns, learning to move *through*, and healing through acceptance and personal reprogramming.

When you come to think of your desires now – with your breathing slow and constant, with your distracting emotions and day-to-day thoughts muted – note whether they seem "natural" considering the flows of time and space or if they happen to force things that aren't ready or willing to be. Are these hopes and goals really feasible or do they demand ripping, pulling, or tearing in order to be achieved? What are you really hoping for yourself too if the latter is true?

Sometimes what you consider to be helpful for your anxious nature actually confirms it and makes it all the worse. In some cases like this, the very things you're doing to make yourself "better" are holding you back from any healing. If you do have trouble going with the flow and constantly force yourself through or into situations based on what you think you need, it's time for a reality check. Here, now, as you breathe deeply and consciously, consider how it might be *fueling* your anxiety to keep forcing things to happen in ways that combat what wants to naturally flow around you. Here, now, with patience and love directed both outward and inward, consider how you might be pushing so hard that you're causing yourself stress and pain.

If you think you might truly be working in detriment to natural cycles and hoping for too much, first things first — go through your desires with a reality check. If it seems like your whole world would have to shatter for a certain desire to be achieved, you'll likely be better off rescaling that hope to be more achievable sooner. Additionally, if it seems like you'd have to be a whole new person for a certain desire to be achieved, you could benefit from reexamining whether the hope is actually good for you *now*. Be honest with yourself in this important moment of self-analysis. When you're ready and you're sure that your desires are healthy, achievable, and productive, simply visualize them in your mind.

Go back to that imagination space behind your eyes and visualize your desires as you want them to be, visualize yourself achieving those goals, visualize how you will feel after you've gotten them, and visualize how your life will be changed. Through this imagination-based process, you invite the natural laws of the universe to attract what you want and inherently work in your favor. You choose to radically reject patterns in your behaviors of control-seeking tendencies and you allow yourself to stop fighting against what only wants to see you grow.

As someone who's often anxious, you choose to reexamine your value of waiting. It could be the case that waiting normally causes you extreme discomfort and internal tension. It could be the case that waiting actually makes you have panic attacks when it goes on for too long with no conceivable end in sight. Waiting, however, is a completely natural occurrence that happens for *all* living things.

Waiting can be meditative, too. It can give you the opportunity for self-examination, to reality-check, and to ground yourself, but it may still be anxiety-causing for now. Once you re-think waiting in and of itself, you can use it in completely new ways. For instance, rather than forcing your goals to happen through actions that aren't exactly well-timed, you can try actively waiting for the *right* thing to happen. See how waiting benefits you, and let go of your needs to force or control time with each exhalation you release.

For the future, remember to consider the value waiting provides. Try to think of it as providing blank-slate moments to your day when you can inject a little meditation, a little necessary self-healing, a little positive spin. Give yourself permission to hold space for your healing in these moments. Give yourself permission to turn things around for yourself. Don't be too stingy to forgive yourself, too. Anxious people are often *extremely* hard on themselves and it could be their intense desires for control and their high standards for themselves that keep their internal tensions constantly high. It could be, too, that anxious people expect to be able to just *change themselves* for the better.

By expecting to *force* things to *naturally* be expelled from the self, anxious people buy into entirely paradoxical, impossible, or contradictory logic. Instead, you can choose to open yourself to your deeper potential by examining what does and does not work for you as it happens to you. As you come to know yourself better, you'll see those unproductive feelings and urges will fall away naturally and your indifference toward these sensations in the first place will be essential for their dissolution later on. Instead of forcing natural patterns, *expect* them to flow as they will. Instead of forcing yourself, *allow yourself to grow*. Give yourself permission and you'll be surprised by what can happen.

III: Calm the Chaos

As an anxious person, you're particularly attuned to the power of chaos. Chaos is a bitter, omnipresent, and often overpowering adversary in your life, for its presence reminds you how far complete control really is from your experience. Chaos behaves interestingly as a presence or in situations in general. It will always happen, to some extent, but when it does, it draws all attention its way, holds that seat of power, and leaves everyone affected when it leaves.

As an anxious person, chaos is like a vacuum to your energy. Even more so for you than it happens for the average person, chaos zaps your energy and can steal your thunder completely. Chaos simply behaves that way for you and part of the reason for this style of interaction is how *you* respond to the presence of chaos. Of course, chaos is omnipresent – it will not and cannot go away for it's inherent to the nature of the universe. Every experience has its oppositional and balancing experience, so all synchronicity and flow deserve their equivalent balance of chaos. Given that chaos won't be going away anytime soon, it will certainly be you who has to adapt. To make things a little easier, this meditation will present a four-step process to help you do just that.

First, know how chaos makes you feel. Essentially, if chaos were a "trigger" to you, completely altering your day and sucking away your happiness, consider how that triggered response would look. If things got so out of hand you could hardly think, what elements of chaos would have to be present for that situation to exist? Consider the nuances of chaotic situations on your happiness, your flow, your day or even your month, your mood, your patience, your style, and your capacity for kindness. Recognize these pieces of evidence for your relationship with chaos and then we'll use it to your advantage.

Second, invite a space for increased capacity for patience. Based on how you know chaos – or simply losing control – makes you feel, try to imagine what you'd need to be a little more capable around this unstoppable force in the future. Imagine that empty, silent, still space behind your eyes that you established and felt through once more and consider what it would take to maintain that composure, that link to this pure inner space, amongst some of the most chaotic times you've ever gone up against. Invite that space into your life.

Perhaps, for you, this space will be maintained through conscious and meditative patience practices during chaotic moments you come up against. Perhaps, you will establish new and creative defense mechanisms! Perhaps, it will look like carrying a small music player and turning on songs that cue certain emotions whenever you get overwhelmed by chaos otherwise. Perhaps, it will look like stretching for you and you will take a mental step back when you encounter these chaotic moments by extending your neck to feel some relief, relaxing your shoulders, stretching your arms and legs, and more.

Since you are so easily driven to feel anxiety, the stress caused by chaos can bring you intense physical symptoms of discomfort, tension, and panic. This space you plan into your routine to protect yourself will end up providing immediate and needed relief when you go up against all the worst the universe has to offer. Whenever you need to connect to this peaceful inner space, start off by breathing as consciously as possible. Practice active and compassionate patience with the situation and everyone involved, and then breathe your way into your inner sanctuary.

Third, practice an attitude of active acceptance as well as everything else you've been working on in this segment. It may seem like a lot, but it will become almost second nature in no time. As you breathe consciously at this moment and hear these words, you have chosen to be patient and open and receptive. You have already done and learned so much! You have been able to connect with your serene, silent inner space, and you now work on growing your potential, boosting your powers to be able to handle the world a bit differently. In your search for increased potential, you will need to perfect and work with active acceptance on a daily basis.

The more you adopt this attitude of conscious and purposeful acceptance, the more you'll become capable (mentally, emotionally, and personally) at handling anything the universe or others throw your way. In that internal and serene mental space we've been talking about, you hold the potential to shift your overall mentality. Once you're ready to do so, you can adapt constant acceptance as a gesture of healing and patience, and if you need to, *give permission* to yourself to allow this shift. Some overly anxious people are driven to be almost compulsively critical of their surroundings and circumstances, which causes them to force natural laws, timelines, and order, thereby causing themselves undue stress on top of what fate and the universe determine. Through active and conscious permission and acceptance, you'll find the intensity of chaos fading away by the day.

Fourth and finally, visualize yourself literally flying above any chaos if nothing else works. Before you're completely changed in response to chaos, you'll need a way to disarm its intensity on the go. Especially when that chaos happens to be an interpersonal conflict rather than just bad timing or everything going wrong at once, you'll need a foolproof strategy that packs quite the punch. Through an active meditation visualizing yourself with wings or as a bird, you can practice attaining a bird's eye view of any situation. Through this higher perspective, even just lived in the imagination, you'll both emotionally remove yourself from the situation and invite more patient, more understanding logic to assess it when you return. And when you do return, you'll be surprised how small that chaotic moment really was in the grand scheme of things. When you return, you'll be informed and ready for appropriate, forgiving action.

IV: Realize Your Path

Something else that might be causing your constant anxiety could be your progress in life as a whole and how chaos gets incorporated into it. Some overly anxious people are always a bit distracted thinking about all they've accomplished, their current stage in life, and how the two correlate with one another. With all their high expectations and low thresholds for irritation, people who get anxious easily won't respond well to a life that's not going the way they've planned. Of course, this feeling can arise for several reasons, even for the highly anxious person. Life could feel unrewarding, it could feel frustrating or entrapping (as when the individual is stuck in the wrong job), it could feel unfulfilled, with the individual's true potential untapped, and it could feel a variety of other ways all leading up to the individual feeling he or she has failed in some way.

To help correct and heal that feeling, you can try to ascertain *what* in your life is so wrong that you feel so unfulfilled and with that information, you can quiet yourself, discover your true path, and reprogram yourself to align with a healthier, productive, enlightened life with the least amount of anxiety possible. To begin with this mission, make your first step two-fold — re-establish deep quietness and connect to that inner safe space just like you did to disarm chaos in general just a moment ago.

Reconnect with this peaceful inner place by making sure you're breathing evenly, deeply, and steadily. Let any distracting or unrelated thoughts fade from your attention and let any emotions or concerns come and go with the shifting focus of your mind. Switch that focus to your breath and let it only change as your breath does, going inward and blowing outward, in cycles again and again. Through this respiratory focus, you build your inner quiet and make a gateway into your sanctuary.

Along with this quiet, open space comes answers. When these answers to unspoken questions come willingly, as if bubbling up from the emptiness of the universe to greet you, you work against your urge to force and still succeed in your most earnest endeavors to grow. When you receive guidance in this way – from your higher self, spirit guides, God, or otherwise, without force – you will see a path revealed before you that's truer than anything pressured to exist could ever be. You gain the ability to use that guidance to follow your natural path, aligning your life with natural timing without the woes of fear, panic, and force.

As you work to receive these types of answers, something that can help is visualizing a path when you come to your quiet inner space. With eyes closed, go into your imagination – the same inner space that you call your sanctuary, the one that's right behind your eyes – and come to see a path laid out before you. This path could be in the woods, into a city, on a mountaintop, in the desert, at the shoreline of a beach, or anywhere else you desire, but you can't quite see the end of it, that much is certain.

As you look out at the path, you have an innate feeling that will lead you to the answers you seek, even if you didn't voice their respective questions out loud. Still, the universe knows. Your questions are assumed to relate to your potential, your abilities, and your life mission, and when you imagine you set foot on this path in your quiet space, you know you're going the right direction for replies and you feel eager. You sigh with relief and undoubtedly trust that your mind will lead you to the answers you seek.

While you seek to define this calm, quiet inner space and attempt to visualize your path and follow it in your mind, you may struggle and many will do the same. Your inclination for the past long while has been to fight natural cycles of time and force progress when things don't feel quite right. Your urges in this sense have worked against your instincts for patience and slow growth, but you can still get there! Many highly anxious individuals will want to rush this process, but visualization is hard work for even the skilled meditation practitioner. The purpose *is* to have trouble, to work through it, and to get stronger. The *purpose* is to learn and grow with all the ups and downs that entails. As you work through this struggle, be persistent and just don't give up! If you're ready for (and/or *need*) these answers from the universe or from God or your higher self, keep trying at visualizing this path. Keep following it whenever you have a still and silent moment. Keep learning from it whenever you can.

In time, you'll find yourself having an easier time of adapting to chaotic situations. You'll find an increased capacity of being more patient with yourself, with others, with uncontrollable situations, and your progress with life overall. You'll find, too, that letting go of what doesn't serve you becomes simpler, more second nature by the day. Just keep at it! Keep following your path, keep asking important questions (whether aloud or silently), and keep your eyes on the prize — your own growth and development through these increasingly anxious times. Remember — this too shall pass.

We earlier discussed the importance of practicing active acceptance while resisting the urge to force things along, but something else you can incorporate into your daily practice would be the active practice of letting go as well. Let go of your attachment to distractions whenever they arise and let go of the old ways that used to mean so much to you (but that worked to upkeep your incredible stress on yourself). Let go of what doesn't serve and replace it with new practices (be they meditation-based, respiration-based, mantra-based, action-based, or otherwise), new patience, and most importantly, more spaces to grow, thrive, and blossom.

V: Make Space for Health

As a highly anxious person, you surely know of and trust the connection between body and mind. When you overly stress out about something or let anxiety get the better of you, the body and mind demonstrate to you that they are clearly linked and fueling one another to a terrible extent. Meditation works to both strengthen the connection between body and mind as many says. Yes, this is true, but it is not the only side of the story. Meditation also makes it clear which experiences are which: body-or mind-based or in other words, which experiences come from which realm primarily.

With your practice of meditation, you enable yourself to harness the powers of your mind more easily, with goals intended to enact long-standing healing for your body and soul. Through a five-minute-a-day meditation practice taken over even just a month –without any necessary or substantial mantra, visualization, guidance practice, or otherwise – your body will demonstrate benefits that are clearer to you than sunshine. For now, it will suffice to say that you'll have lowered blood pressure, sustained and healthier heart rate, decrease in headaches or migraines, lessened muscle tension, healthier digestion, less-paralyzing fears, and more restful sleep. And these benefits are just the tip of the iceberg.

Ultimately, it comes down to this — through meditation, you work to heal yourself. While the specific practices of this guided meditation have led you through visualizations and affirmations for success alongside additional, varied techniques, there are still a few more methods that you can put in your meditative toolkit for the future. Along the lines of using visualization to your advantage, you can actually make requests of your healing to the universe through meditation. If you can assess what you want, analyze what it will do for you, and express these things to the universe, you might be amazed at what comes back to you.

Because you know that anxiety has lived, embodied, real-world effects for everyone but especially for you, you likely know what areas of your body are affected the most, too. You surely know where you hold the most tension and how chaos affects you differently based on the circumstances and what you've already gone through that day, week, and year. Focus on these trouble areas (or troubling processing systems) in particular. Diagnose their issues and think of what could be changed to be healthier or more productive. Think, too, of what change would look like and what change is most ideal. Let this specific information inform the healing you seek.

As you learn what in your life needs the most help and you begin to direct your energy toward that healing, you will put part of the responsibility for your growth off onto the universe. By letting go of force and the urge to control, you radically accept that things will happen on their own time, even the healing of your own personality or your overall stress cure.

You *can* relax! You can loosen those joints, release a little tension, and shake off some pressure. You can trust that the universe will begin to respond in line with the requests you've made. The reason why you can believe and trust in this gesture is a little thing called the Universal Law of Attraction. When you meditatively focus, breathe consciously, and call out for things to fill needs in your life, you activate this law which dictates that the universe cannot *help* but respond accordingly when ripples of desire are sent out. Believe in your gifts, send out your wishes, and allow yourself to truly trust in the power of waiting. These are the steps to visualize and actualize your success.

You can attract your own healing and you can connect with something larger than yourself. Through the gift of meditation, you can breathe consciously and direct your power towards anything you desire, be it sanity, stress-relief, serenity, stability, or anything you could imagine. When it comes down to it, your power is dually held in two closely-related realms — your emotions and your breath. If you believe, trust, and have faith – if you feel openly and peacefully – while you breathe consciously, you can command your world.

Through this practice of unfolded, conscious breathing, you allow yourself to take healing energy into any imaginable area of your life (or others' lives). The limit is only defined by what you can imagine and what you decide is worth your energy. Make sure your limits are as low as possible when you begin meditating by making sure to breathe *into* and *through* any tension whenever it arises. Just like it's problematic to force what you want, it's equally wrong to ignore a truth or opportunity that you know aligns you with your goals. Don't deny yourself just because you're afraid. Go for it because you *know* it is right.

When you experience stress, whether out in the world or within your own body, always remember to breathe into the experience. And then keep breathing until you're through it. It's important to know that when you hold your breath and limit your respiration in moments of high anxiety, you deprive yourself of oxygen, you decrease your potential, and you engage in biologically self-defeating behaviors. From now on, refuse to limit yourself in this way. Accept your potential, draw out and follow your path, and then see what the future has in store. Chaos be damned, for growth is all that matters now and you'll wait as long as you need to for it to become actualized.

Guided Meditation for Anxiety and Kundalini Awakening

Meditation for Kundalini Awakening

Align Your Chakras, Awaken Your Third Eye, Become More Confident, Find Inner Peace, and Heal Your Soul

I: Gather Your Energy

As you prepare yourself for this meditation of kundalini awakening, come to a comfortable position. Whether it's a seated, standing, or reclined position, gather yourself and collect your energy for this moment. Allow yourself to slow down your active, everyday self. Allow yourself to connect with the deeper and more cosmic energy of your soul. You'll have to calm down that everyday self, of course, before you can make any giant steps. So, let's begin there.

In your comfortable position, close your eyes gently. Don't tightly shut them, just let gravity pull them down and let yourself look at nothing as they come to close. In that dark space behind your eyes, let your imagination take control. Let your thoughts come and go at first and get a sense for their speed, their themes, their focus. Let any emotions filling you up simply be present and as you're able to, let yourself come to terms with that presence. Look around in this space behind your eyes and notice what's going on inside you. Go past just this mental realm too, go down slowly through your whole body to give a systems check to yourself.

Move from your mind to your nose, your mouth, and your throat. Do you feel any congestion or pain here? Any bad feeling or simply free flow? Move down then to your shoulders, your chest, your heart, and your lungs. What's going on deep within? Is there any distracting tension? Do you have any pain or discomfort here? Any excitement or over-working? Or simply free flow? Move down again and out to your arms. Are they sore or tight or stiff, or do you hardly feel them hanging there? Are your hands numb or ready for action? Down to your stomach, your abdomen, and your hips. Are things okay here? Do you feel any tension or discomfort, perhaps from indigestion or malnutrition in some way? And even lower, in your pubic and genital region, how are things feeling? Are you comfortable with yourself here or do you have traumas attached that aren't able to be discussed yet? In your legs and your feet, how are things flowing here?

As you conduct this internal assessment of your body, try your best to breathe deeply and as evenly as possible. Try not to hold your breath at any time, but if you happen to do so, note which area of the body you happen to be scanning at the time and think, too, of what that link could mean for your overall health. Your innate pattern of breathing has a lot to say about what's going on deep within. Do you breathe deeply and evenly always or do you have issues with holding your breath and not even knowing it? As with a bit earlier, do you hold your breath only when you encounter certain problems or when you think about certain things? Try to learn more about yourself through this bodily assessment – through your breathing flow, your tensions, and your painful places. Look deep within and prepare yourself for what's to come.

With your eyes closed and your breathing sure and steady, with your internal state in check and your goals on the meditation at hand, you must now establish your center. When you investigated those bodily spaces before, you likely felt how your consciousness can move to different regions of your body at your command. You hopefully felt how you can bring all of your attention to your stomach area with practice, or to your throat or your third eye and imagination space. In this case, you'll bring all your energy and attention into a space you'll define as your "center."

Your center can be wherever you feel it should be and for now, let that central place come to you intuitively. For you, is it in that behind-the-eyes space? Or is it in your heart? Your diaphragm? Your gut? Where do you feel your energy circulating around as if it was an energetic vortex within you? Wherever your consciousness is pulled, let this space be your "center" for now and then breathe into that space. Breathe deeply, giving energy and life to this area, dissolving any tension and letting any thoughts or feelings about it come and go like mist evaporating in the sun. Breathe attentively and let your inner awareness come to life.

What you're noticing when you built up your center and when you breathe life into your body is your kundalini. What you're noticing when you quiet your thoughts and still your mind to a peaceful emptiness is your kundalini, too. The cosmic energy that pervades daily life is kundalini and it lives reflected within you and within me, too. Within all of us, this uncoiled energy waits to be awakened so it can dance with the universe around it and when you look deeply into yourself, breathing as consciously as possible, you allow the universal energy within yourself to arise and acknowledge *itself*.

When you spent time noticing each realm of your body, you performed important work related to the healing of your kundalini energy. Sometimes, this energy can become corrupted by imbalances within us. Sometimes, we can lose touch with our kundalini entirely by distractions in everyday life, but the kundalini still rests in wait, coiled up in the pits of our stomachs, curled up around the seats of our souls.

When you did that energetic assessment earlier, whatever areas you felt in pain or tension will likely later (or now) be areas of imbalance, where blockages are keeping your kundalini energy from flowing freely. As we move forward, what you noticed then will demand that you grow strong enough to heal that weakness in the future and you needn't be overwhelmed or afraid. Simply know this healing is coming. The abilities you need to succeed are readily housed deep in your core and you wouldn't be here if you weren't equipped for the ride.

II: On the Kundalini

The origins of studies on the kundalini come from times as early as 1000 BC in Hindu tradition, where historical records indicate the importance of the energy science and the spiritual philosophy behind this particular aspect of creation. According to the original studies, kundalini refers to the spiritual energy we all contain that's located at the base of our spines. This spiritual energy itself is referred to as Shakti, but kundalini is the great potential all living beings have to become aligned with that godly, universal presence.

For these early practitioners – and for kundalini scholars, students, and practitioners today – the kundalini was described as snake-like. It was physically described as a serpent and the actions it completed as a vessel of energy within a living body were then commented on in theme. That coiled up energy at the base of the spine would unravel and dance like a charmed snake through the basic energy wheels of the living body and then the snake would reach the crown of the body and turn back down, establishing a flowing serpentine motion through the body, hitting every major internal energy center on the ways up and down in order to trigger awakening.

Literally, the word "kundalini" derives from a Sanskrit word that hints at something that's small and coiled up — in this case, the presence of "God" or source energy within all living things. Metaphysically and spiritually, kundalini suggests that we can unlock our godly potential and come to live purer lives through both knowledge and guided meditation. The knowledge required first relates to some of the smallest and most important vehicles of energy in our bodies. First things first, the knowledge required necessitates an understanding of chakras.

As you breathe deeply at this moment and feel centered in your body, ready to learn and grow with this meditation, remember those realms of the body we walked through before. Recall those places of tension, the place of free flow, and the sensation of finding your "center." What we were really doing in those moments was taking a journey down through your chakras to assess the general state of things.

As we move forward with this meditation, keep this even pace of breathing and visualize along with the information being shared with you. In your body, there are seven places where energy is pushed through your body. These seven places relate to seven glands of the human body – those small and important energy vehicles in the body – and seven energetic "chakras." Literally, chakra means a wheel or disk that directs the flow of energy. Each of these chakras is spaced at different parts of the body, but all along the vertical line of the spine. Starting from the base and moving up, these energy wheels help us process emotional and mental complexities related to these bodily spaces and they work to keep the overall vibration of the body flowing in harmonious balance.

The kundalini reflects on how the movement through your chakras is going. It asks how things are going for you deep within and it posits that health problems or imbalances of other sorts easily arise when things are not going well but remain clearly avoided. The kundalini requires a degree of self-awareness, to that effect, although the kundalini and its potential still exists within every living body. The more cognizant and driven you are in your practice, however, the better.

When you meditate on the kundalini, it awakens bit by bit. When you meditate *to awaken* the kundalini, it responds immediately. Your coiled-up snake then shivers awake and quivers into the warmth and starts going about its business with a little more urgency. As the snake starts to move, it will begin at the base of your spine and move first through your Root Chakra which is all about survival and links to the color red. As it moves through your Root Chakra, it will provide healing and balancing godly energy to your feelings about sex, intimacy, and overall security.

The snake will then move up into your Sacral Chakra, which is all about creativity and links to the color orange. The Sacral Chakra will experience the blessings of this rising snake through increased inspiration, vehicles to let out their creativity, and affirmations that they're supported and loved. Moving onwards, the snake will go through your Solar Plexus Chakra, which is all about willpower and links to the color yellow. As the serpent moves through this chakra, it will remind you how to say no and what's worth saying yes to.

Moving up to the Heart Chakra, which is all about love and devotion linking to the color green, the snake will make you question your relationship to *love* itself as well as what might be blocking your ability to love. As the snake moves on upwards, it encounters the Throat Chakra, which is about communication and links to the color of light blue. Here, the snake will encourage you to examine how your words are used and what their consequences are. Then, the snake moves through the Third-Eye Chakra, which is about seeing beyond sight and links to the color of dark or indigo blue. In this region, the snake's movement helps you realize what you might have been missing or unintentionally blind to.

Finally, the snake will move up and through the Crown Chakra, which is all about connecting to the higher self and links to the color purple. In this sphere, the serpent helps you align your life with your greatest potential and opens you up to messages and gifts from the universe. After the snake gets to the top, however, it turns right back down and goes through them all again before going right back up to the top. The kundalini within us is relentless when we invite its awakening. It wants us to open up and connect with the source, with the divine.

The kundalini runs on your trust, devotion, and hope. It runs on your commitment and determination too, for your commitment to these meditations will certainly help your progress along more than would be the case without them. The kundalini works to get your energy flowing and then you get to see what falls in place around that healed-up core. Through practice, conscious breathing, and the desire to access your higher awareness, in time you *will* awaken your kundalini and begin on your path to enlightenment.

III: Your Inner Truth

Look back now on what you noticed before with your trouble spot (or spots!) and imagine that you can see that area (or areas) surrounded by the color of the nearest chakra. If you're having issues with your reproductive area, (desires to have children without the ability to do so or recent or long-past trauma, etc.) then envision that you can see deep beneath the skin to the trouble spot and the area is surrounded in a warm, red bathing light. If you're having issues with your heart – not feeling loved or feeling like you have so much to give but no one to take it, etc. – look deep into your heart and see that area bathed in warm, forest green light. You get the picture.

Find that trouble spot and look deep within. Look directly at it now, with the intention of healing. Breathe consciously — slowly, deeply, quietly, and constantly. Breathe into that space and see that colored light glow brighter. Imagine that you can feel the kundalini at your core – the snake that lives along your spine – starting to move and wiggle its way to the same place that holds your attention. As it moves upwards and downwards at a steady pace, it hits this trouble spot twice each cycle, once on the way up and once on the way down. With this constant attention and healing interaction, visualize that the light behind your pain starts to fade from bright red, blue, green, or whatever to pure and simple white.

Look into that space of turmoil and see your attachments to it fade as the light changes tones. Look deeply and realize that what so many people have said across time is true — you can't rush perfection. Since you know what you want in terms of healing, let's have you try something new rather than angry hoping or pressured affirmations. Let's have you make yourself as emotionally neutral as possible as the kundalini snake keeps making its rounds. Let's have you become quiet on the inside, less distracted, and fully open for anything. Let's get that snake moving and then we'll learn to vocalize what you really want.

While you're looking deep inside yourself still, with neutral feeling towards your body and your trouble spot(s) now, test yourself. Feel this serpent move over your trouble spot and you know that space is being purified, pumped-through with godly or source energy. Trust that healing is happening without you trying to force it. Now, with strong posture, internal consciousness, and a positive attitude about healing (but no emotions otherwise), begin a chant of your choice.

When you think of what you want for your awakening, is it purely bodily? Are you looking for joint healing, glandular healing, or otherwise? Or is it purely spiritual? Are you hoping for an increased connection to the divine and further gifts to amp up that relationship? Is it a mix of the two, perhaps? When you think of what you want for your kundalini awakening, there must be some words that come to mind. As you complete this visualization with the snake and your trouble spots, begin to speak aloud these words until they become like a chant.

For kundalini energy raising, chanting works incredibly powerfully. When you repeat over and over what your soul truly needs, the universe can't help but respond, but also, in these meditative moments with this type of repetitive vocal practice, your kundalini energy will find itself awakened all that much easier because you can put words to your hopes – because you've aligned your voice with the goals of your higher self. That alignment activates so much potential.

If you need to take a moment before moving on to brainstorm a little more direction for your kundalini awakening, that's absolutely understandable. In all actuality, it's probably a smart move to define your goals and check them against your higher self first, to make sure they're aligned with the growth you really need, rather than just what you *want*. So, let's take a moment to brainstorm. Gather a piece of paper and writing implement or a nearby screen with a note-taking app. Get those ideas flowing.

Start off with physical goals just to get ideas out. What bodily healing goals do you have? Better joints? Easier digestion? Increased strength? Fewer allergies? Then, move on to your emotional goals if you have any (and the kundalini hopes you do!). What emotional growth do you hope to achieve? Increased empathy? More friends? A real, loving, intimate relationship? A change of pace in life? Finally, look at your spiritual goals. Are you hoping for increased psychic abilities? More spiritual friends or perhaps a guru or a teacher? Are you simply here to awaken your kundalini? What else is going on with you?

When you've been able to write out all the potential goals you have, see if there are any common themes throughout the list. If you've written a bodily goal of becoming stronger and an emotional goal of learning how to say "no" better," then your overall goals as a person (on all three bases: bodily, emotional, and spiritual) seem to align with increased strength. Focus on that when you perform these kundalini meditations and focus on the solar plexus as your "hot spot" or "trouble spot" for you need a little core work to get your energy flowing in tip-top shape once more.

Once you have all these hopes and goals written out and you've been able to define or pull out any themes or overall standards in your passage toward growth, you'll have a much better time establishing your chant or mantra. With that added verbal boost to your meditations as mentioned above, that kundalini snake will have added direction and the verve to get things done. Through just a touch of brainstorming, you'll enable your advancement to be faster, more thorough, and even more long-lasting.

IV: Visualizing & Making Space for Awakening

Let's get into the meat of this meditation now. With the information you've been provided with, you know what the kundalini is, how it works in the body, and what it wants to do for you. You've also assessed what it is you want for yourself and how to filter out desires that have lesser importance. Your familiarity with the kundalini will be increased exponentially now and forever more, for your awakening will be put fully underway in a matter of minutes.

If your overall awakening seems to take longer to play out in your life than you've hoped for, the most important thing is to be patient and understanding with yourself. In these cases, practice active and radical forgiveness, acceptance, and appreciation of yourself without any adjustments or energetic shifts. Sometimes the kundalini energy within us can tell we're forcing something and it will make us wait to realize that before it allows us to blossom. Sometimes we need to change our diets to become more receptive to this transformative energy. Sometimes we need to start practicing different meditations, different sports, or different activities in general to gather information first before the kundalini is ready to become engaged. Sometimes, we need to wait, and that's absolutely okay.

If you find yourself meeting a blockage in your development and awakening potential, take a step back and consider *why* this might be happening. Your ego may be a bit too loud.

Guided Meditation for Anxiety and Kundalini Awakening

Your internal imbalances may be taking command. Your goals may not be as pure as you think. Simply take a step back and reevaluate. If everything seems on the up and up after your examination, keep up the good, meditative work, and the universe will surely respond in time. It'll just be more so on the *universe's* time, rather than your own.

When you're ready to move forward, see yourself in your own mind's eye. With those eyes closed and your breathing deep and steady, visualize yourself in your own imagination. See yourself sitting in that comfortable position, breathing deeply, and finding your peace. Note how strong and secure you look, how dedicated and how relaxed too. Then, see yourself surrounded by a powerful white light. This light seems to emanate from your skin and it glows like the sunrise. As this light fills the space around you, you feel certain of your higher nature and feel affirmed in your purpose with this guided meditation.

As you look at yourself sitting and breathing in peaceful meditation, make sure you are both sitting with strong posture to validate the work your core and spine are about to do. In real life and in your visualization, start to engage in your chant or mantra once more. Speak about what you want to attract into your life and what you will gain from your kundalini awakening. And visualize that the light becomes brighter around you with every repetition of your chant that you vocalize.

Promise yourself to the world. Promise to that world and to all Shakti surrounding you that you will say "yes" from now on as much as possible, for the sake of this divine connection. Promise yourself that you will do everything the universe points you towards, for you know that your process of awakening doesn't stop with these 5-to-10-minute meditations. Promise to devote yourself toward the generative, creative, and supportive force of the universe and feel that snake at the base of your spine starts stirring, start awakening its motion through your chakras.

As the snake awakens at your Root Chakra, visualize the light around you (that is the light around yourself in your imagination) turning bright red. See a smile grow on your face and intuitively feel that this imagined-self feels assured, protected and safe, and therefore happy. As the snake moves up to the Sacral Chakra, see that light turn deep and glowing orange. The smile lingers on your face, but you know that this time it's because you feel inspired and ready to create art after a long, long dry spell. Moving upward, the snake tickles your Solar Plexus Chakra and you laugh aloud as your surrounding light becomes yellow like sunshine. You know that your confidence and strength of will fueled that laugh rather than the serpent's tickle.

As the snake moves upward, it activates your Heart Chakra and your surrounding light becomes this brilliant shade of green. Your smile becomes deeper, a little wider, if that's even possible and you feel love exuding out in ripples even just through your imagination. Next, the serpent licks your Throat Chakra, turning your light a simple pale blue and your smile reflects ease of speech. You look like you could burst out into joyous song at any moment. Then, to your Third-Eye Chakra, the serpent coolly climbs, making your light shine deep indigo rays from your skin. Your smile suggests calm knowledge and insights gleaned through senses other than the standard 5, and finally, the snake swirls into and through the Crown Chakra, turning your surrounding light a peaceful and glorious purple. Your smile expresses truths divined from source energy and reminds of those often found on ascendant masters across time.

Now, visualize that the snake starts to move just a little faster. The colors of your surrounding light change much quicker too and before long, the snake's motion turns you into a rainbow blur of color. Eventually, with calm and collected breath on your part, the serpent begins to move so freely that the rainbow colors create a haze of simply pulsating white light. Feel the lights that surround you in your imagination being forced through the prism of sped-up time, revealing their true nature as pure white healing light all along. You were always working toward kundalini awakening, you just helped to speed up the process! The knowing, connected smile you see on your own face is constant and you sense that nothing can harm you. You know that awakening is nigh.

This awakening will follow you out into the real world where you're constantly posed with important and unspoken decisions. This awakening will encourage you to act differently and engage with others in completely new ways in support of the growth that's to come. In that case, you'll definitely want to say "yes" to anything that piques your interest or that serendipitously points you in line to your goals. Trust yourself, trust the universe. Keep your head on straight and breathe deeply. Your transformation is just around the corner!

V: What's to Come

In your process of kundalini awakening, there will be a handful of hard times and strange side effects. There will be glorious moments and there will be breakdowns. When you work to unlock this awareness of your internal energy spheres and their impact on your overall health, you will experience intense fluctuations before any sort of enlightenment can be reached. You might even find yourself changing and shifting in appetites, desires, and potential before you settle in your new self.

Awakening is always a big moment and it's not just good things that will happen to you – well, it's all for the good, but some of it might be uncomfortable. Awakening often involves detoxing as well, which can mean irrational, stinky, moody times ahead. During awakening, you might feel like your path is revealed more clearly or that you have a greater sense of direction, but you could also have to live through frustrated, listless, isolated, and directionless moments in order to get there.

When you awaken, you'll undeniably have a stronger sense of yourself, as you exist in this dimension, as well as how you exist on higher planes as a self (or soul) connected to God (or source energy). During your awakening, you will feel full of self, you will hear your inner voice more clearly, and you will feel overwhelmed with new direction and potential. When you're ready to get to this point, you will know, and once your awakening begins, you should have no doubts about what's happening inside of you.

As far as what you can expect in your kundalini awakening, let's start with the emotional complexities. Your breathing and consciousness now will help you feel less out of control in response to anxiety, stress, and frustrations later on. You will have increased sensations of openness, acceptance, purposefulness, and joy. You may even feel blissful more often than ever before. You may still have extremely low-energy days and you may still go through periods of intense sadness or depression, however, once full awakening is achieved, you will not be able to harbor these types of emotions for very much longer. You simply won't have space for them alongside all the rest of your abilities and strengths.

Emotionally, too, you'll become vibrant with buzzing energy and creative urges. You'll have rid yourself of any momentary blockages to any of your chakras so you'll be flooded with pure source energy at this time. You'll feel that something you've been longing for has been achieved and your aura will surely be affected. As you breathe in this moment, consider the future at your fingertips. Consider your chances at healing and energetic awakening and let yourself feel hope and confidence that these moments truly are coming. Through this conscious attraction, your meditation will create your new world.

In addition, when you're in the throes of kundalini awakening, you'll feel lingering traces of feelings and emotions from years and years ago as your body forces you to process what memories haven't fully healed in you yet. Your body will speak in volumes as you detoxify and develop yourself anew. You'll need to work through certain things to get into a full awakening, so if you find yourself spontaneously bursting into tears or having hot flashes, erratic outbursts, or angry tendencies, you're going to get through it. Remind yourself these things need to happen, they need to get out for you to be cleansed and opened to the universe.

Now, let's look at some of the physical side effects that you may experience during this awakening process. At first, you'll likely get energetic ripples through your system that feels something similar to anxiety. While your energy is getting rewired and repatterned into a healthier consciousness and vibration, the shift can be intense. Seek alone time to tune into your inner vibration and use meditations like these to help that shift feel as effortless as possible.

In this moment, where you've found your peace and where you create your future, you breathe and establish your space. At this moment, you awaken the snake of energy within you who comes to dance up through your chakras to your crown and back down to your core. At this moment, you invite awakening and you accept all that's to come. The energetic shifts, the changes in diet and craving, the changes in interest, the overwhelmed feelings, the need to dance or run, the need to slow down and exactly what it is that you really need – these things and more come your way with your practice of clearing and intensifying your power.

Finally, let's see what your end-goal may look like once your awakening is complete. Breathe with the flow of the facts coming your way and feel relieved, warmed, strong, and hopeful about their enactment in your life in the near future. You will know your inner voice well and you'll trust its insights whenever you hear it, for you know this voice connects you to a higher self or guardian of some sort. With the kundalini energy awakened, you will be this connected. You will also have a deep connection to your inner Truth. So many theories of life and world today reject concepts like "truth with a capital T," but the enlightened, awakened individual is earnestly able to tap into their personal truth, the truth attached to their soul and through this connection, they can come to heal any ancestral, personal, or past life ailments that might be appearing in their current self-expression.

With the kundalini awakened, the individual will experience something like a second puberty that unlocks authenticity, wisdom, bliss, and more once the excess is sloughed away. Through quiet, meditative alone time, you will be rejuvenated and inspired to continue. You will come to a place of acceptance and appreciation of your new found gifts and will find emotional obstacles cleared away.

At the final stage of awakening, you will lose touch with the importance of ego-driven things and ways of being. Your pure state of being – as energy – will be the only one of value and the all-demanding, all-distracting "I" that you were will fade away as you realize how connected you are to everything and everyone around you. As you reach the climax of your kundalini awakening, as that snake reaches its fullest ease of movement within you, you will feel yourself becoming One with all that is. Through love, devotion, and practice, you will transcend. You will blossom.

Thank you

Before you go, I just wanted to say thank you for purchasing my book.

You could have picked from dozens of other books on the same topic but you took a chance and chose this one.

So, a HUGE thanks to you for getting this book and for reading all the way to the end.

Now I wanted to ask you for a small favor. **Could you please consider posting a review on the platform? Reviews are one of the easiest ways to support the work of independent authors.**

This feedback will help me continue to write the type of books that will help you get the results you want. So if you enjoyed it, please let me know.